3 4028 07927 3828
HARRIS COUNTY PUBLIC LIBRARY

J 394.261 Dea
Dean, Sheri
Martin Luther King, Jr. Day

$22.60
ocn496610066
02/22/2012

D1218901

WITHDRAWN

Martin Luther King Jr. Day

By Sheri Dean

Gareth Stevens
Publishing

Please visit our Web site, www.garethstevens.com. For a free color catalog of all our high-quality books, call toll free 1-800-542-2595 or fax 1-877-542-2596.

Library of Congress Cataloging-in-Publication Data

Dean, Sheri.
  Martin Luther King, Jr. Day / Sheri Dean.
     p. cm. — (Our country's holidays)
  Includes index.
  ISBN 978-1-4339-3918-1 (pbk.)
  ISBN 978-1-4339-3919-8 (6-pack)
  ISBN 978-1-4339-3917-4 (library binding)
  1. Martin Luther King, Jr., Day—Juvenile literature. 2. King, Martin Luther, Jr., 1929-1968—Juvenile literature. I. Title.
  E185.97.K5D385 2011
  394.261—dc22
                          2010000417

New edition published 2011 by
Gareth Stevens Publishing
111 East 14th Street, Suite 349
New York, NY 10003

New text and images this edition copyright © 2011 Gareth Stevens Publishing

Original edition published 2006 by Weekly Reader® Books
An imprint of Gareth Stevens Publishing
Original edition text and images copyright © 2006 Gareth Stevens Publishing

Art direction: Haley Harasymiw, Tammy Gruenwald
Page layout: Daniel Hosek, Katherine A. Goedheer
Editorial direction: Kerri O'Donnell, Diane Laska Swanke

Photo credits: Cover, back cover, p. 1 Howard Sochurek/Time & Life Pictures/Getty Images; pp. 5, 17, 21 © AP/Wide World Photos; p. 7 Diana Walker/Time & Life Pictures/Getty Images; p. 9 Hulton Archive/Getty Images; p. 11 National Archives/Getty Images; p. 13 © Delphine Fawundu/SuperStock; p. 15 AFP/Getty Images; p. 19 Vicky Kasala/The Image Bank/Getty Images.

All rights reserved. No part of this book may be reproduced in any form without permission in writing from the publisher, except by a reviewer.

Printed in the United States of America

CPSIA compliance information: Batch #CS10GS: For further information contact Gareth Stevens, New York, New York at 1-800-542-2595.

Table of Contents

Boldface words appear in the glossary.

A Special Man

Martin Luther King Jr. was born in 1929. He died in 1968. King worked hard to make sure everyone was treated the same.

4

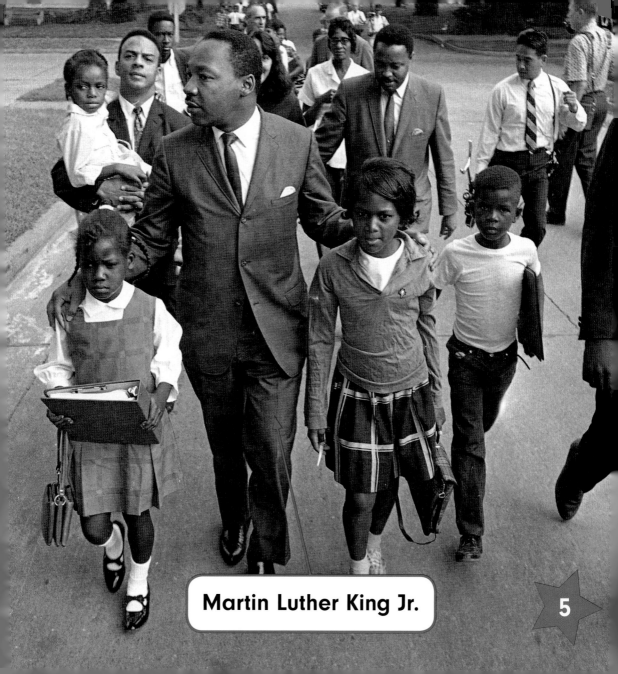

Martin Luther King Jr.

A Day to Celebrate

In 1986, President Ronald Reagan signed a law to honor King's life. It said the third Monday in January would be Martin Luther King Jr. Day.

President Ronald Reagan

7

As a boy, King saw that all Americans were not treated **equally**. White people and **African Americans** were not always treated the same.

In some places, African Americans had to live in their own parts of towns. They could not go to the same schools as whites. Some could not even vote!

His Dream

King had a dream. He wanted everyone to live, learn, work, and play together.

13

Martin Luther King Jr. gave **speeches**. He talked to many people about his dream. He led **peaceful** marches to help make his dream come true.

Martin Luther King Jr.

Martin Luther King Jr. did not believe in fighting. He knew that hurting people would not help his dream become real.

KEEP
THE
DREAM
ALIVE

17

Martin Luther King Jr. helped change how people thought about each other. He worked hard to make sure people were treated equally.

19

On Martin Luther King Jr. Day, people write about King. They give speeches. They draw his picture. People think about how they can help others, too.

Glossary

African American: a person of African background who lives in the United States

equally: in the same way

peaceful: without trouble

speech: a public talk

For More Information

Books

Bader, Bonnie. *Who Was Martin Luther King Jr.?* New York, NY: Grosset & Dunlap, 2008.

Rappaport, Doreen. *Martin's Big Words: The Life of Dr. Martin Luther King Jr.* New York, NY: Hyperion Paperbacks for Children, 2007.

Web Sites

Martin Luther King Jr. Day
holidays.kaboose.com/martin-luther-king-jr-day.html
Find out about Martin Luther King Jr. and his day.

Martin Luther King Jr. Day
www.holidays.net/mlk/sitemap2.htm
Find links with facts about Martin Luther King Jr.

Publisher's note to educators and parents: Our editors have carefully reviewed these Web sites to ensure that they are suitable for students. Many Web sites change frequently, however, and we cannot guarantee that a site's future contents will continue to meet our high standards of quality and educational value. Be advised that students should be closely supervised whenever they access the Internet.

Index

About the Author

Sheri Dean is a school librarian in Milwaukee, Wisconsin. She was an elementary school teacher for 14 years. She enjoys introducing books and information to curious children and adults.

24

HARRIS COUNTY PUBLIC LIBRARY
HOUSTON, TEXAS